My Voice

To Mrs Vera Harwell,
Thank you for your love and
continual support in everything.

Samuel Singh.

by
Samuel Singh

authorHOUSE®

AuthorHouse™
1663 Liberty Drive, Suite 200
Bloomington, IN 47403
www.authorhouse.com
Phone: 1-800-839-8640

First published by AuthorHouse 5/10/2007

ISBN: 978-1-4343-0795-8 (sc)

*Printed in the United States of America
Bloomington, Indiana*

This book is printed on acid-free paper.

Introduction

For the past few years as I was writing these poems I had the idea of portraying Guyana in all the beauty and splendor that I know it possesses. I then realized that if I were to do such a thing, I would be lying to myself and the audience I was writing for, so I decided to be true to myself. I knew that there was a lot of good in my birth land but there was also evil prevalent. The land has seen great struggle in the past as well as a violent history from which the Guyanese people have not really recovered or forgotten. Thus, the themes of the poems changed drastically and I worked with a renewed burst of energy that I never knew before. It was my understanding that there were stories to be told, viewpoints to be expressed and a definite stand to be taken, so I took it, much to the disagreement of others.

This book is a collection of works that happens to laud; people, places and historical figures. It is a voice for; protest, nostalgia and narratives and others. I mentioned my 'Maa' twice within this book and she was not my mother but my maternal grandmother who passed away. She was someone who I greatly admired quite the same as my other grandmother. Both of them are strong matriarchal figures who attract nothing but love and respect when people think of or meet them. I had also mentioned Gavin Narine, whom I'm sad to say was murdered in Guyana in October of 2002. There is a striking contrast between such atrocities that occur and the love that a person can still show to the land of their birth.

Within the pages of this book are pages of poetry of different categories but ultimately the universal theme; Guyana. There are poems that are; narratives, odes to places, philosophical and fantastic, nostalgic, of people and of protest. As you can see there is an encompassing mix of ideas and thoughts that have come into this book and I am most certain that there will be something for everyone.

Let me also take this time to mention that I take no political stand or allegiance and those who know me can testify that my views are my own. On that note, I hope that you would find my poems enjoyable as well as food for thought. Enjoy them.

Samuel Singh

Acknowgements

I would be amiss if I didn't thank those who helped and encouraged me on the writing of this book. Both my family and my friends played a very important role in helping and supporting me to write at times when I felt discouraged. My sister Sarina was constantly telling me that this book should have been completed a long time ago and it's hard for me to say she is ever right on anything but I agree with her. I would also like to thank a good friend Navin Prashad and who was kind and instrumental enough to find photographs for me. There is also Bibi Saliema Brehaspat who sent photographs of her recent vacation in Guyana. Without the help of these two people, there would be no decorative and thematic pictures present and for that I am grateful.

Dedication

This book is dedicated to the one person
who has managed to keep me true to my
belief that I can be a poet and writer (often times
with reverse psychology). It is with sincere love
and appreciation that I can dedicate this book
to my sister Sarina.

Knowing
Nostalgia

Guyanese Flavour

Born to be unique
be a gentleman
Guyanese twang on my lips
destroyed by precise language,
English standards,
but, designed by chutney and calypso
now forcing transformation into ballroom dances
of proper steps.
But, there remains
too much tassa in my heart,
too much curry in my stomach.

Listen!
"Very good to meet you sir,
A pleasure indeed."
Understand?
Crisp and precise,
unfeeling.
Now say,
"Wha happenin Star?"
Properly polluted
with culture coming back.

See Pundit Balram there
with dhoti wrapped with seven curry
standing in *wok house*
singing in Hindi :
"*Ohm bur bura swaha,*"
and a little boy giggling;
"*Me nah know dah swaha.*"
Youth, the firmest, overwhelming
with proper broken English.

Soon trouble arrives,
Mommy sees and says;
"Skin teeth does end in
Cry!" punctuated by a slap
on the head back.
Tailor made English for the occasion
"Pandit, yuh word dem
inspire me,"
smiles the woman
while little boy tearfully massages
his head back.

When all is said and done
we have two languages;
A Canecutter who says,
"me chap till me han sore
an a snake wha been deh
Me chap he rass too."
Followed by a little boy who
asks, "Ma, a wha dah?"
followed by GT boy in second English;
"Da is whot?"
Followed by visiting child
from Queens, New York
"Mom, what are they saying?"
A third English?

Three English,
three tunes,
three boys,
One heart.
Yet hear me saying
on the telephone;
"Yes Boss, we'll do that,"
Followed by
"He rass mad!"
After hanging up.

Proper on the surface with
Guyanese twang burning within.

Home Grown

A cast net tries to trap old dreams
abundant with words and ideas
from rural into
urban existence, yet
old times, nostalgic memories and emotions
drain through the net,
too fluid to be caught.
Happiness, is the freedom of
infinite mango sweet thoughts
is the courage is swimming
with an alligator.
Companions and friends mourn
things passed.
My treasures are never for mourning.
There will always be a new
experience; older than me
newer by the years.
Remember; Phagwah, Eid, Easter
and Christmas?
I reminisce with
grown men
grown strong
grown in age
always children at heart.
The best of life always remain
Home Grown.

Secretive Stumps

You stumps of time
now standing rotted and petrified
amidst the high trees who
filter sieve like sunlight
on an off beaten path
far from the intruding eyes
of civilized men.
Here, in the jungles of Guyana
you groan and rustle
phantom leaves of memories.
Tell me what your utterances are.

I stand among you in
dank decaying leaves,
snaking vines and fallen twigs.
When I die, your roots
will find their way to me,
so speak I implore.
What are you saying?

They will send my lifeless husk below
cushioned by your leaves
and embraced by your roots.
My spirit will sing with yours
over treetops with birds,
on the ground with jaguars
and give you hope like jungle rain.
But, speak while I live,
what are you saying?

You might be whispering of
Dutchmen who came as settlers
pale European men exploring your forests.
you may speak of Englishmen
camped at your base
seeking El Dorado.
Or, do you tell ancient secrets
of Amerindians hunting and
stalking soundlessly among
you and your brothers.
You may speak of everything;
historical, physical and spiritual to
those seeking to hear.
So tell me trees,
tell me what your utterances are.

Narratives

An Immigrant Thought

No well traversed path by identifying name
bought such people from, 'The Land of Many waters,'
Yet, it manned a Guyanese into an American dream
to write this history to be seen

Drunken Creativity

We congregated and they poured me liquor
from a wide assortment.
There was poetic anger
and lyrical lynchings.
Yes, and we
refilled out cups.

They told me about lines and verses
from learned Greece to now, spoken word.
We even clashed on art
And enjoyed the interpretations
From Da Vinci to Picasso.
Yes, and we
refilled out cups.

We spoke of history; Guyana and Europe
like Hadrian's wall clouding my vision.
They raved and craved-
pondering philosophy,
and we laughed at Confucius.
Yes, and we
refilled our cups.

We chopped at Chaucer
and sneered at Shakespeare.
They laughed at Peter Kempadoo's beard and hair
and reinvented the protests of Carter.
In the end we resolved to write better than they.
Yes, and we, as always,
refilled our cups.

Worried Man

Dew drops of tears you see
and you inquire why I stare
up into the blue vastness.
You ask of my; learning
                    yearnings
                    work
                    aspirations.
You ask why I stare.
I will mention to your ears
though my Mother and Father never heard
I release my words to you.

Men make families and some
like my Father; toil in earnest,
raising children
in this commercial age
where money melts
when placed into their palms.
            He has bills to pay,
            a family to provide for,
            needs food to eat,
            clothes to wear,
            children attending school.
They grow to see the hardships
            accept them or do different.
They grow and graduate from
one suffering into another.

Now,
your ears burn with the why
and you watch me stare.
You heard.
I see visions adorned with flaws
because,
the altar in my head
longs for; prayers with the good and
the abundance
of creativity
to share
       regardless if it feeds me.

       Dawn to dusk I see faces
some similar to me, most not
working in offices and streets,
most in despair, like the street harlot
selling sex and seeing survival.
I persevere
       a man starved
       to seek just once chance
       To now feed my Father.

People

Maa

Your physical remains lye on a pyre
and ceremonious oil and flowers are scattered
on the wrapped small frail figures that served
inspiration
to this inquisitive heart.
I remember your stories of;
Moongazers, Dutchmen, Bacchu and the Sugar Estate
where you were acquainted with hard work.
Small in stature yet large in perspicacity
I grieve with others now you are home,
suffering ended
fiery consummation beginning.
It reaches and blazes you to ashes,
but, sparks remembrance not forgetfulness
of heatedly calm words of wisdom.
Within small minutes you return
"Ashes to ashes, dust to dust,"
and while not present
Yet, I saw.

My Maa's Experiences

Maa always spoke of experiences.
Maa's very fiber was of experience.
At evenings on our landing
Maa would rest her fragile body on the steps
and weave the magic of her experiences.

Dark coolies
working in the sugar fields
and black people and coolies
waiting for the estate truck.
Of wives; washing clothes,
cutting rice with a grass knife,
cleaning cane fields
and singing bhajans.
Maa's voice was strong as her hands once were
leaving my imagination with stories,
bringing shadows and open spaces to life
With her experiences.

And I would listen and ask questions
knowing that Maa's experiences were real.
I knew that Maa never forged her experiences
from books she couldn't read
but, that they were pages
from that book that was her life.

I would stay quiet
on those dark evenings
And listen to my Maa's experiences.

Gavin Narine

Gavin Narine's
depart
    a master who drove
    a blood red and mournful black
        racing car
eating speed and leaving the competition blinking dust
             Marvelous
family and life loved him
           now kindly answer us this
why did you strike him with bullets
Murdering Animal

Chacha Canecutter

Chacha Canecutter
Me like how yuh cutlass sound
how it sing and chop cane.
Me a go talk yuh story.

Me see yuh wid blade an hook stick
in wan green bush o sugar cane,
cutlass a raise and cane a fall.
Sun a shine hot hot and place heat bad
till yuh muscle cover wid plenty sweat.
Yuh know wha fuh do, cause yuh a do am long
fling an swing a cutlass blade
and whistle one ole chutney tune bout rum
as cane a pile up; plenty, plenty
when yuh hand a pass am.

Chacha
Me does watch how yuh a walk wid power
chop fuh send sugar abroad
Wok fuh give yuh family food.

Uncle,
yuh hand an cutlass a wok
nuh fuh estate quota
but, fuh yuh pickney
who deh in primary and high school.
Sugar good and pay nice
but, nuh fu yuh pickney.
Dem got fuh mek dem life
and learn from book.

Chacha,
me watch yuh everyday
And praise yuh strenght
but, yuh nah know.
Yuh wok hard in big backdam
hook an chop an pile in punt
like slave and coolie dem
does do long time back.

Yuh heart beat like tassa drum
one tune wid thousands
wokin fuh Guyana soil.
Me know yuh pray in mandir
yuh bow yuh head when
bell ring, shell blow.
Yuh ask fuh strength,
prayin fuh God bless yuh.

Chacha
you neva wok in vain.
Me been a watch yuh fuh years.
See how me respect yuh fuh long time
an me honour yuh
wid dem words dis.
Me Chacha cane cutter.

Market Woman

That woman, thirty pushing fifty
squatting on the ground, legs folded,
selling fish displayed on an old rice bag
every market day for years
has also known the carefree days of youth
until the necessities of life
hardened her olive skin into dark brown.

Praying Vagrants

I stand and distinguish that vagrant
remembering durations when I saw more
at a stelling in New Amsterdam bound for Rosignol.
They emerge in all encompassing ethnicities,
outreaching dirt stained hands,
eyes reinforcing perished honour and pride
now pleading assistance.
Their clothes, long lost of colour
all reflecting their earthen beds
and smelling of baths long forgotten.
With an aching heart you know
that splatter of age;
many children, maturing
amidst a habitat of squalor
within lands where pity
resides in the bosoms of those
who still retain a conscience.
Where are the ones who utter
of economic instability while
lining paid-off pockets with the money
of hard working citizens?
Is it fitting for us to see
people pleading charity while we
veer away?
Do you know that they are attached to
our own family

of humanity?
How are you able to turn your face
from those like us;
begging because they cannot work,
have no lives,
no family,
support
to call their own?
Why do we earn
and bestow to bewildered politicians
who rely with no reluctance on promises,
while, after election and endorsement
rationalize why they were broken and
never attempted.
Unfortunately, many of the homeless we pity,
pray for
gnash their teeth, shake dirty, dusty feet
and throw vile, vociferous voices
loaded with contempt and curses
at us.
What do we
spectators in this world
think of this?
We are human
some humble
some dependable to and unwittingly make
mistakes,
demonstrating a morbid awakening that

not everyone happens to be on the corresponding page,
not all love,
not all want help.
Some want liquor, rum,
want money from the youth sent to beg;
brother or sister, daughter, son, child
sent revolving amidst the beggarly streets.
Insane, insufferable, yet, intensely ironic
is it not?

Little Beggar Boy

A boy walks and I cannot understand
what I feel when he passes.
He is a; dirty, malnourished beggar
who calls to me without a word.

He carried nothing but, the money in hand
seeking more from those who pity.
But, this smart child smiles and roams
as if he was richer than all.

My Teacher

He who was a teacher
    was a leader
    was versed in the disappointments
        and triumphs
        of a single day of
        learning and chalk dust.
He is no longer there.
He migrated after sufferings of;
    retrenchment, losses and
    saw hope flicker out.
Teacher happier but,
    children without quality leadership.
The land is ripe, yet there are
    errors in causes
    cowardice known as boldness
    and a lack of workers
        for the fields.

Protest

Keep Vigilant

Don't sleep! Form the vigilante squad,
share the cutlasses and guns.
No one will disturb my village tonight.

Look at me; dressed in black
holding a cutlass
gun in pocket
bullets in another
beckoning others to join.
Death will greet the thief,
the killer will die.

Houses nestle people
sleeping in fear
fearing they may never awake.
Children will fear no more
purification is coming
people are waking up.

Unrecognized

This I do know;
  yesterday's Elysium is
  today's purgatory is
  tomorrow's underworld.
    Heaven or hell
    it is Guyana.
The drink
trembles in my hand,
drunkenness
soothes my mind.
I understand this land
  less today
  than yesterday
  unrecognizable tomorrow.

Ghastly Jewels

Prisons await the hellish scaremongers, they
        who dispense; death, thievery and cowardice.
Open ears await a politician's vacuous promises, they
        who speak; slander, lies and preach condemnation.
Rum awaits a poor man's tongue, it
        intoxicates and chases is predicaments for a moment.
They cry to everyone
        man and God.

God has forgotten this land of;
        prisoners, politicians and poor.
                Paper bars await political prisoners.
                Apprehension awaits those seeking a living.
The entire parcel is
        bundled in barbed wire
                and worn as a necklace by all.

Mr. Sweet Talk

Look inna he shine eye
and hear dem nuff nuff word dat
a come from he mout dat a lie.
He can gyaf up people me a tell yuh dat
and wen yuh see im, he telling bout sumting new.
10 year now dem a mek bridge
but all dem a do a read book bout book wha write
but you know, one, one dutty does mek dam.

Dat blagghad Naag, come in mandir
and eat food and nuh giv
any a dem people who want am.
No. Dem a siddung an laff and get fat
from abbie wok wid sweat, blood and eye wata,
Now yuh kno wha mek dem smell like renk meat.

Dis one heh fuh PPP and PNC,
all de time dem a mek promise fuh bring moon
since abbie get mo blackout dan currant.
We need de light fuh de pickney read
we want dem fuh larn mo dan we
Nuh fuh sen yuh baytah a Oxford an Cambridge from
we money
Dat yuh fuh mek we road.
Dis a me story a declatation
dat get a tune
wat come frum de hungry bellie an de dyin lady
dat a lay down inna de street an front yuh house.
Well "Mr. Elect," sufferin nuh always come in
Politics dat read 'oppostion party influence.'
Yuh tell dat to de muddah who bubbie
Dry. She pickney die.

Wha bout dem flood wha come?
Yuh seh dat yuh a giv de bess fuh yuh bredda dem
but we see clean wata inna yuh drain wile
we gat fuh drink de dark kala pani mosquito wata yuh
leff fuh we.
Is whe we clean wata deh? In yuh house?
Me tink you tink it good if yuh get am fuh
We benefit.

We barefoot school chile get feva
an me nah get money fuh medcine.
Me a cry every time me a see dem
hungry, hungry bellie dat groan fuh food
and de mout wid foam a carna and bus up wha leff
a brite line red.
Yuh see de muddah?
Me hol she han but can't tek all de problem.
Now wen we ask fuh help you a drink wine and talk
"Nonsense, we have perfect social and economic
structure."
Me a still wait fuh yuh get sum structural.

Yuh kno me wife sell she tilarie
wha been in she family since she muddah, muddah time
so we can get food fuh eat and mek safe?
De shop nah even giv trus
so me can pay bak. But...
wid wat?

Now "Mr. Sweet talk" we nuh barn inna de one same
country?
yet, you mind deh sumwhere else
an nuh pon we like yuh should.
You a talk bout national pride and a wear
Diamond ring an
catapilla suit.
One day. One day, hungry bellie guh mek nuff nuff noise
an even empty barrel go come and roll
fuh yuh full am.
Yuh up deh a tink bout dear, dear ting
and me stand heah and a talk
Bout poverty problem yuh bring.

Confession

If I could create with calamity,
pellucid calamity,
I, also would be victim to
chaos,
disturbance,
the hate.
I ponder to myself
amidst the hate in souls,
I confront the birthing dawn
eulogizing
in my working class way.
I'd shoot my orations to them
like poison
to decimate
or, if not,
I'd place my hands on their heads
with blessing
to purify
my loathing with theirs
inspecting
blood
knotting a tie
on their smiling necks.
If I could create with calamity
I would sooner die
than be diplomatic and speak

to them,
becoming
a heir
not to Burnham's
racism,
and Cheddi's ideas of
communism.
If I could create with calamity
pellucid calamity,
I'd burn the rioters, killers down
and pen my poems
from the ink
of their ashes.

A Guyanese Pleas For Peace

Dispersing themselves, rioters have rioters
as the gangster has competition
and me my thoughts.
Peace is not a matter of life alone,
it seeks unification and rises
beyond politics, race and creed.
It entreats the;

> courage of the religious,
> strength of the laborer,
> nurture of the mother and
> directness of the father.

I acknowledge my words as your read them
hoping you perceive them as they are heard.
I loathe that I still have to record them,
reminding men that we are human
and our brother's keeper.

And though villainy and anarchy seek to
slit out throats, drink our blood to
fuel its forbidding passion, it fears Peacemakers.
"Blessed are the Peacemaker," we are enlightened
with others hoping we dedicate hour lives for
peace and our fellow man.
Others are us and
we are others.
Let us earnestly exert ourselves
for what we pledge;

> dedicate our energy
> and use our literacy,
> for the pursuing propensity
> of peace.

Elegy Of A Country

Above flies the Golden Arrowhead
in the Guyana breeze.
Underfoot is the lush land,
pregnant soil.
Perilous is the land of Guyana
      in three counties
      in the politics
      in the core of violence.
God save me! I love Guyana!
God save me! Crimson is my blood
identical to the gun waving killer,
      as his eyes scan me,
      down the barrel of a gun
         in three counties
         in one land.
Within the pregnant soil
Mother Guyana acquires;
      coffins
      ashes
stifling her matriarchal love
being buried with her children.
This ought to be a time of rebirth,
      with the same Golden Arrowhead flying
      in the same breeze
      in a new way of thinking
      planted in the same soil,

but, with no meaning,
purpose.
The sugar cane; succulent and emerald
green and good with its own story,
harvested once by slaves and laborers
now by free men.
How many know they are emancipated?
Day and dusk pass
under the enslavement of fear,
fear of a bullet
and death.
Daylight brings tears and burial
night brings the mourning
of Mother Guyana
for her children.

My Beautiful Land

This is a beautiful land, sweetheart.
See the snakes crawl,
ready to give a doglike lick of poison,
then, you see the wild animals
      to adore.
The bright sunlight glows lustily
over hibiscus flowers adorning
the gravesites of the murdered.
This a beautiful land, sweetheart.
See the changing seasons of
      plentiful;
            from robberies, rape and riot
            to political animals
            and anarchists.
A spectacular circus with
fools and ignorance in control.
It is a parade of cowering fear,
Innocence lost, never to return.
      Do you see your citizens
      armed with automatic weapons
      that lovingly take lives?
It is a rebirth of; thugs, hooligans
smiling in the blessed Guyana sun,
shooting unborn futures and
cutting threads of human lives.
      But, this is *still*
      a beautiful land,
      Sweetheart.

I Hear The Dead March

I head a guitar
with human veins for strings,
and a harmonica
of ivory from dead man's bones.
The music was bloody;
notes carved with a knife
with a beat supplied by gunfire.
Loud melodies mingled with suffering,
only silent in a tomb.
Animals roam and trees grow peaceably
but, we understand each other with the
compassion of a trigger finger.
The song sings
tuneless and melodious
secreting into our flesh
marking us
for the time we hear it
No More.

Fruits Of Violence

The roti non-existent is hot
waiting for the imagined butter to melt
while sipping bitter tulsi tea
sweetened by teardrops.
The hunger hurts,
the stomach swells while
limbs and flesh waste away
Bringing to fruition a breathing skeleton.

My Song Of Freedom

Scoundrels of Satan
cower in Guyana.

      Buxton, do you harbor killers?
      Lost are the times when
      Indo and Afro Guyanese
      lived, breathed and died
      in peace with one another,
         in Buxton.

The riots of the 1960's
      confiscated that life.
      Now you harbor the abominable.

Do you remember,
      "Am I not a man, and a brother?"
         Brotherhood fought for.
         Brotherhood earned.
         Brotherhood dead.

Killers! Be careful where you step.
My forefathers;
      Cuffy, Critchlow,
      The Enmore Martyrs,
      Rodney and Carter
         all cry as you step on their breast.
         you kill their teachings,
         desecrate ideals.

This is not the life they sought
for sons and daughters of Guyana.

In these days,
scoundrels seeks to rule,
killing the dreams of my ancestors,
opportunities for the future.
Although gunmen boast with bullets
walking like heroes;
Barefaced Snakes!
Though they hate and target my words,
I hold my head high
and like Carter,
"I clench my fist above my head
I sing my song of freedom."

The Gold Of El Dorado

Imagine Atlantis,
full of wonder and technological bliss.
Remember Egypt?
A cabin of history in mankind's ship.
Let your mind wander to Babylon
with lush hanging gardens in the sun.
Now, travel to the land of the Greeks
who gave democracy, legends and lush feasts.
If you still wonder of riches untold,
there is El Dorado, city of gold;
found in Guyana, ancient in years,
olden young and polluted with fears.

i ask

mystic old lady in a hammock
smoking a cigarette
eyes a faded ring in her hand
gazing for the future

obeah man with a handful of dust
sipping rum in a cemetery
tosses bits of bone to unfurl
things to come

young lady sips delicately
from a decorated silver cup of tea
looking at the arrangement of tea leaves
seeking a sign for tomorrow

psychic gazes in a trance
at a crystal ball
shuddering uncontrollably
as a ghostly voice whispers the future

i sit in my study
reading news of yesterday
politics crime greed and i cry
asking the knowledgeable ones to share
when would guyana find peace

Stagnant Changes

Show me changes, dissimilarity
and a I'll show you stagnation
as life drip drops
to our pace on life's path.
My disquieted thinking labors
during the same midnight hours
and I find no relief.
T'was last week I dreamt
I rested a pickaxe within a brother's head
understanding he would have done likewise.
Repulsing, to my disgrace God refuses
to interpret the signs I pursue.
A brother
a son
a father
have all died before
but, this one by my hand.
Though mine was fictional
I felt more at more guilt than the godless ones.
Stagnant changes still remain.

Sacrifice Of Hens

Loud, with cackling and pecking
they feast on bugs in a backyard
amidst coconut trees and grass and leaves
reeking their chickens smell in my yard.
They seek simple living
as we look upon them in hunger.
They perch upon medusa like guava branches
at night.
Prey for greedy fingers.
They disappear, perish
And we wring out hands
grievingly thankful it was only chickens.

Places

My Birthland

The place of my birth is forever my homeland
from the Rupununi savannahs to No 63's red sand.
Tis a fixed vision to reminisce about the Port
Mourant Market,
and playing in Albion Complex the phenomenal game
of cricket.

Memories flood my head of Corentyne Comprehensive
High School,
of teachers, debating and proper educational tools.
That High School life was the most unrivaled I had
involving; sports, academics, social life and a
one ton school bag.

Our bush cooks in the coconut farms of Tain were wondrous
even though we transported everything by hand generating fuss.
These are memorable tokens that are easily adored,
like the buckets of water we carried to use or store.

May I never disregard from memory waiting at the
New Amsterdam stelling
and watching the brown Berbice river water with fishing
boats, vendors selling
after which I take a back seat in the Rosignol bound boat,
to behold the churning waters and feel the boat sway as
trucks enter with a beat.

I recall riding a bicycle and chatting with friends in the
afternoon light,
watching girls and whistling to see their faces in anger or delight,
then racing to a friend's house as dusk approaches
bringing mosquitoes as we burn coconut shells to deter
their touches.

There were nights in Belvedere when frequent blackouts
would materialize,
and we sat in moonlight on benches, trading jokes and
those idolized.
In front of the yard a small group fills the air with laughter,
while others join and the gathering swells with joyous chatter.

Soon, someone brings a kerosene lamp and a deck of cards
silence prevails while watchful eyes place silent bets
hoping for grand rewards.
Electricity returns and angry murmurs now rise in protest
and the game is now moved into the backyard with
friends, company of the best.

Scenes such as these are too numerous and unique to be
forgotten
like; riding to the Pay Office market at Williamsburg
for fresh mutton,
then, stopping for crushed ice and ginger beer just to cool off,
and pushing the bicycle through the market browsing
and hearing idle gaff.

I remember fondly of walking hand in hand wit my sweetie
and dodging suddenly in the schoolyard so the teachers
never see her with me.
We often sat in the canteen and spoke of things beyond us,
and recall nothing except the girl while going home on
the mini bus.

Sadly but truly, on the Corentyne are funerals of
different magnitudes
like; the Madrasi drinking and dancing with loud
drums and joyous attitudes
while, in Philippi you are transported into a cowboy country,
and a Guyanese vaquero goes in a procession of horses
and rough beauty.

My homeland is a place rich in history and culture,
So much that each settlement has stories laced with
sadness and rapture.
Each is acknowledged for uniqueness; Barima to Corriverton
making me proud with adoration.

The land that brought me also taught me many things
mostly good and some never honorable making their
thoughts sting.
Natural disasters are averted but manifested in people
who live for disturbances and chaos, a diet, staple.

We need to see each other as a family who share the same land
just as our forefathers who worked and prayed hand in hand.
We ought to be educated from the past to safeguard the future,
So a change of brotherly love would true and mutual.

Seawall Tune

The Atlantic's rowdy barrage clashes with stone
against a wall of incredible length
blocking waves.
It stands firm; a monument of the land.
If the seawall could speak;
defiance, defense and dedication
would coat its words.

It had seen; British ships,
cargo vessels, fishing boats.
It has felt the lash of the waves
both tempest tossed and
calm massaging waters.

For decades people have;
walked, ran, strolled and caressed each other.
The seawall knows.
It has seen history made
and lovers in the act.
Its experience is miles and
knowledge encompassing the Guyana coast.
It sill watches Guyana today and
want to speak to the people
the stirring tales it knows.

Forgotten Graves Revisited

A Kiskidee in a tamarind tree
sings mellifluent for no one to hear.
Its loud sharp voice resounds in the air
from a perch in the graveyard green.
Bleached headstones of a hundred years
overgrown by bushes and covered with moss
are the only remnants of who once were.
An off beaten dirt track winds on forever
behind a tiny village settlement
nest to open green space close to the ancient sea
among other tracks from various times and eras
ending at the cemetery.

Sea blue skies and slothful clouds overhead,
cadavers of people down below,
who were once workers of the land.
among the burial mounds and tombs
vines embrace concrete crosses and Hindu flags.
Time is passing
many are forgetting
and the land is recreating
memories of who had passed,
who viewed history;
      indentureship, slavery
      freedom and independence.
Imagine if their stories could be told.

Envision the life of ancestors
viewing Château Margot and Dutchmen,
traveling across the Atlantic in
the Whitby or Hesperus in indentureship.
Picture the sting of the whip,
cry of slaves, the songs of spirituality
that came from their lips.
Their blood had built a nation,
their cries reverberate today
of a life in bondage and plight for freedom.
Now they lie interred here,
from rice fields, cane fields, slave quarters and logies.

Your bones lie
one with the soil again,
the same land you worked for
now part of it.
The Kiskidee salutes your memories
singing to your holy legacies
the only way it knows how.
You hoped your children's children abiding today
retell stories of when you were strong
printing your name for generations to come.
You want them to recall your sacrifices
and abide in a land now their duty to keep.

But, how many remember a livelihood of struggle
legacy of lashes and times of torment?
You sleep with ship brother and slave worker,
powerful and respected, a respect earned
by droplets of weary blood and spilled sweat.
You may be forgotten forevermore
just another unmarked grave.
But, understand,
the Kiskidee still sings for you,
the land embraces your body
and a lone figure cries
thanking you for your sacrifices.

Once A Home Now A Remnant

I live in a house now non-existent,
forgotten after its laden foundations, I went
without sign of human presence but the earthen floor,
a floor with holes for awara seeds
and a little boy's eager muddied hands.

Within its unbuilt fences the animals graze
from the dusty streets to ear the green, always.
The guava tree forgets it fruits
since none climb its branches or caress its roots
along the length of drain where any waters seldom flow.

I see, melancholic hearted
shards or memory not yet departed
in that house that I grew up and abandoned.
Beyond the dust bathed road and cracked asphalt,
night arises and I hear no bats at play.

Leathery flights flutter no more
since I forgot their lodging above the old church door.
I hear them dance with the evening swallows
forgetting the parakeets talking overhead.
I've forgotten it all to remember it now.

Under the moon glow and distinguished stars
I've forgotten the sandlfy stings and mosquito scars
within the dark and polished verandah,
of wood I've forgotten I helped to arrange
home, where I lived, now seemingly a wonder.

The house remains, inhabited by forgotten memories
comforting each other and excluding my misery
with the forgotten songs I used to sing.
And I view this fabricated real sight
only to forget it tomorrow.

My Home-Belvedere

Late afternoons at home
dusk smothers the light resurrecting mosquitoes
that plaster onto us like tiny droplets
of black rain swelling with red.
    My blood is in the land.
Birds dart in the dark
        with breathless winds
        scissoring tails
        sharing the skies with bats
        flying ferociously free.
It is their home too.

They are of the dusk
seeking darkness,
living by fang and beak
with mosquitoes seeking nourishment
they come; servants of twilight,
older than those who reside there.
Each eve is the reenacting of a ritual
High in energy and fluttering frenzy
that demonstrate things I no longer can;
    They love their home.

Berbice River

Water; brown and silty, flows
    pregnant with dirt and sediment
    certain of its Atlantic path.
    crystal black waters
    from the mountains, estuary bound
    past jungles; green with leaves, feathers
    growling with life.
    Past caiman nests and alligator holes,
    dancing with river otters,
    turtles, piranha and arapaima.
    Brown; mirroring life,
    invaluable land, people, the creatures
    and just as rich.
Flowing freely forward past men,
    haunts of men,
    past Cuffy's historic home,
    fetching canoes to Amerindian villages,
    waving at bauxite mining,
    embracing logs, sawmill bound.
It enchants those who seek and dare;
    to be rich
    to be adventurous
    to be destined for
    dominion or disaster.
What does this river see?
    everything; dried banks

to flooded forests.
It has tasted
blood and ore
gold and gore,
brought life and death,
provided and taken away.
We normally get mesmerized by its waves from
New Amsterdam or Rosignol,
bushes and silt on its shoulders
logs in its arms and
ships across her back.
A rich man's pride,
poor man's living,
and a country's river
named Berbice

Brooding At The Berbice River

Ever go at the stelling at New Amsterdam
on Saturday to savor cane juice alone?
Ever sit by the docks entranced
by the river wondering
what more life has in store?

Ever mull over family;
abroad, at home, alive and dead?
Ever wonder of women
you loved, left and wished
never existed?

At the stelling on the Berbice River
        Saturday
        afternoon
        with cane juice
        alone!
I once wished I was abroad or dead
thinking of who would know
if I went.

Philosophy
And
Fantastic

The Claim

I saw the old Higue leap
then the Bacchu peep
from the nearby Dutchman
under the tamarind tree.

    Soon, they young old woman walked
        cobwebbed gown glowing,
        face; bottomless black;
           playing a flute
           with ghostly tunes
           and chorused by owls.

They stink of Death,
calling for another companion
across the street.

    Within the dark house
    silence prevails, then;
    a wail,
    a howl
        rises from the living
        as a man of mist
        walks away with them.

Dreaming Reality

In my sleep I saw my native land
once hopeful.
Soil oozing with life,
trees indicating with each other
aiming at the sun
Wallaba and Greenheart like sentinels
sentries of the land.
On the meandering coast
flowers blossomed and
courida bushes stood guard.
Kiskidee and Blue saki
spoke with blended voices
no man could replicate.
A humming bird
darted in the fragrant air
for nectar in a thousand bouquets.
The waters bubbled in
brooks and flowed in rivers;
This land of many waters.
The sight seduced me
and I went there
to be enfolded by the greenery
sheltered by the skies.
Then, I awoke
tears tainted my eyes and
I wept at my loss.
My paradise was no more,
it was touched by me.

Learning Lillies

An old fishpond houses
lotus flowers and water nuts trembling
in a sea of lily leaves
distributed like empty plates facing skyward
umbrellas to fishes below.

Aquamarine lily leaves embrace
creation under the heavens
nesting fishes in their shade.
  Offspring are bounteous;
  water nuts for children,
  pink lotus flowers adorning the waters
  and the likeness of Lakshmi.

Be placid like lilies,
  open to ideas
  provide help when needed
  and accept children as
  God's gifts.

Bothering

It seems the things that make me think
and bother me profoundly
have no weight with you.
So, I'm going to keep writing
till they bother you too.

Lost Land

Living in a world full of politics;
where individuality is obsolete,
we see lives revolve around economics,
and the production and movement of shuffling feet.

The leaders of men now control life,
and with it comes negativity, hardships and strife,
for the simple reason that our sagacity fails to see,
our lands are loosing their spirituality.

About the Author

Samuel Singh was born in 1981 on the Corentyne coast of Guyana, South America where he spent his childhood. The family then moved to Jamaica, West Indies where he lived for four years where he found a love for writing. He retuned to Guyana in 1996 where he completed High School and all the while he developed more of a passion for creative writing and poetry. In 1999, he moved to New York with his family where his father currently works as a Lutheran Pastor. He graduated from Queens College CUNY with a B.A in Media Studies and English. Through the sought critique of other writers, he has kept perfecting his craft. Mr. Singh places a lot of emphasis on his roots in Guyana and is proud of that fact and tries to remain widely read on Guyanese and Caribbean poetry and literature. When asked how he has the ideas for his poems he says, "The ideas just come to me and I write it down. During the process of writing it takes a life of its own and upon completion I always thank God for giving me the ability and the inspiration to put these ideas down."

Printed in the United States
79128LV00001B/253-348

9 781434 307958